A TREASURY OF PRAYERS
FOR NOW AND ALWAYS

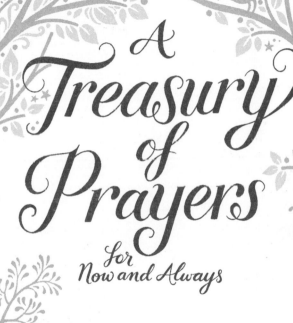

A Treasury of Prayers

for Now and Always

WRITTEN AND COMPILED BY
MARY JOSLIN

LION

Written and compiled by Mary Joslin
Illustrations copyright © 2013
Kate Forrester
This edition copyright © 2013
Lion Hudson

The right of Kate Forrester to be identified
as the illustrator of this work has been
asserted by her in accordance with the
Copyright, Designs and Patents Act 1988.

Published by Lion Children's Books
an imprint of
Lion Hudson plc
Wilkinson House, Jordan Hill Road,
Oxford OX2 8DR, England
www.lionhudson.com/lionchildrens

ISBN 978 0 7459 6347 1

First edition 2013

A catalogue record for this book is available
from the British Library

Printed and bound in China, December
2012, LH06

Acknowledgments
Every effort has been made to trace and
contact copyright owners for material
used in this book. We apologize for any
inadvertent omissions or errors.
All unattributed prayers are by Mary Joslin
and Lois Rock, copyright © Lion Hudson.
Prayers by Elena Pasquali, Sophie Piper,
Mark Robinson, and Victoria Tebbs are
copyright © Lion Hudson.
Bible extracts are taken or adapted from the
Good News Bible published by the Bible
Societies and HarperCollins Publishers,
© American Bible Society 1994, used with
permission.
The Lord's Prayer (on page 123) from
*Common Worship: Services and Prayers for
the Church of England* (Church House
Publishing, 2000) is copyright © The
English Language Liturgical Consultation,
1988 and is reproduced by permission of the
publishers.
The Scripture quotation on page 124 is
from The New Revised Standard Version of
the Bible copyright © 1989 by the Division
of Christian Education of the National
Council of Churches in the USA. Used by
permission. All Rights Reserved.
"We give thanks for domestic animals" (on
page 84) by Michael Leunig is © Michael
Leunig, used by permission.
Prayer by Blessed Teresa of Calcutta (on
page 139) used by permission.
Carmina Gadelica collected by Alexander
Carmichael is published by Floris Books,
Edinburgh.

CONTENTS

FESTIVALS OF THE CHRISTIAN YEAR 173

About Prayer

ASK, AND YOU WILL RECEIVE

Jesus said:
Ask, and you will receive;
seek, and you will find;
knock, and the door will be opened to you.

For everyone who asks will receive,
and anyone who seeks will find,
and the door will be opened to those who
  knock.

Your Father in heaven will give good
things to those who ask him.

FROM MATTHEW 7:7–8, 11

PRAYER AT SUNRISE

Come into my soul, Lord,
as the dawn breaks into the sky;
let your sun rise in my heart
at the coming of the day.

TRADITIONAL

STILL AND QUIETLY

I sit still and quietly
in this, my quiet place,
and think of good and lovely things
and God's unfailing grace.

ELENA PASQUALI

SO STILL

O make my heart so still, so still,
When I am deep in prayer,
That I might hear the white mist-wreaths
Losing themselves in air!

PRAYER FROM JAPAN

THE LIGHT OF ETERNITY

To pray
is to open
the soul
to heaven
and the eyes
to the light of eternity.

A LIFE OF PRAYER

The prayer of speaking
The prayer of listening

The prayer of kneeling
The prayer of walking

The prayer of working
The prayer of playing

The prayer of giving
The prayer of receiving

The prayer of laughing
The prayer of weeping

The prayer of loving
The prayer of forgiving

The prayer of living
Till life's ending.

FAITH

My faith is like a slender tree:
scarce enough to shelter me
from the rain and from the heat;
yet here, alone, with God I meet.

I HEAR GOD SPEAKING

Looking at the sky
while a tall tree sways,
I hear God speaking
in a thousand different ways:
of melodies and miracles
that all are born on earth;
of dreams and possibilities
of everlasting worth.

SOPHIE PIPER

HOPE IN ETERNITY

My world, it is material,
my dreams, they are ethereal;
my days, part of infinity,
my life, lived in simplicity;
my knowledge is uncertainty:
my hope is all eternity.

MYSTERIOUS GRACE

The world is such an uncommon place
in all the vastness of time and space
which some unseen mysterious grace
has made a home for the human race.

INFINITE BEAUTY

I stand in the presence of the infinite beauty
   of the stars.
I stand in the presence of the infinite beauty
   of the moon.
I stand in the presence of the infinite beauty
   of the sky.
I stand in the presence of the infinite beauty
   that will endure
when the stars and the moon and the sky
   have run their course.

HEAVEN'S MUSIC

If you have heard
the sound of birdsong
in the morning air,
then you will know
that heaven's music
reaches everywhere.

IN GOD'S BLUE HEAVEN

A skylark scribbles
brief notes on the art of flight
in God's blue heaven.

GOD'S GRANDEUR

The world is charged with the grandeur of God.
It will flame out, like shining from shook foil;
It gathers to a greatness, like the ooze of oil
Crushed. Why do men then now not reck his
 rod?
Generations have trod, have trod, have trod;
And all is seared with trade; bleared, smeared
 with toil;
And wears man's smudge and shares man's
 smell; the soil
Is bare now, nor can foot feel, being shod.

And for all this, nature is never spent;
There lives the dearest freshness deep down
 things;
And though the last lights off the black West
 went
Oh, morning, at the brown brink eastward,
 springs –
Because the Holy Ghost over the bent
World broods with warm breast and with ah!
 bright wings.

GERARD MANLEY HOPKINS (1844–89)

HELP MY THOUGHTS

God help my thoughts! they stray from me,
setting off on the wildest journeys; when I am
at prayer, they run off like naughty children,
making trouble. When I read the Bible, they
fly to a distant place, filled with seductions. My
thoughts can cross an ocean with a single leap;
they can fly from earth to heaven, and back
again, in a single second. They come to me for
a fleeting moment, and then away they flee. No
chains, no locks can hold them back; no threats
of punishment can restrain them, no hiss of a
lash can frighten them. They slip from my grasp
like tails of eels, they swoop higher and thither
like swallows in flight.

Dear, chaste Christ, who can see into every
heart, and read every mind, take hold of my
thoughts. Bring my thoughts back to me, and
clasp me to yourself.

AUTHOR UNKNOWN

Praising God

PRAISE THE LORD

Praise the Lord from heaven,
all beings of the height!
Praise him, holy angels
and golden sun so bright.

Praise him, silver moonlight,
praise him, every star!
Let your praises shine
throughout the universe so far.

Praise the Lord from earth below,
all beings of the deep!
Lightning, flash! You thunder, roar!
You ocean creatures, leap.

Praise him, hill and mountain!
Praise him, seed and tree.
Praise him, all you creatures
that run the wide world free.

Let the mighty praise him.
Let the children sing.
Men and women, young and old:
Praise your God and king.

FROM PSALM 148

GOD'S GREATNESS

O God, your greatness is seen in all the world!

I look at the sky, which you have made;
at the moon and the stars, which you set in their
places, and I wonder:

Who am I, that you think of me?

What is humankind, that you care for us?

O God, your greatness is seen in all the world!

FROM PSALM 8:1, 3–4

ALL THINGS PRAISE THE LORD

All things praise thee Lord most high!
Heaven and earth and sea and sky!

Time and space are praising thee!
All things praise thee; Lord, may we!

GEORGE WILLIAM CONDER (1821–74)

PRAISING WITH A GLADSOME MIND

Let us with a gladsome mind
Praise the Lord for he is kind;
For his mercies ay endure,
Ever faithful, ever sure.

JOHN MILTON (1608–74)

PRAISE AND GLORY

You alone, O God, deserve praise and
glory, because of your constant love and
faithfulness.

PSALM 115:1

SING A SONG

Sing to God with thankfulness,
sing a song of praise,
sing out loud and joyfully,
sing out all your days.

FROM PSALM 95

SONGS AND DANCES

Praise the Lord with trumpets –
all praise to him belongs;
praise him with your music,
your dancing and your songs!

BASED ON PSALM 150

LET THE WHOLE WORLD

Let the whole world shout and sing,
Let your praises joyful ring!
God has come as this world's king:
Peace and justice he will bring.

From Psalm 98

PRAISE, HONOUR, AND GLORY

May none of God's wonderful works keep
silence, night or morning. Bright stars,
high mountains, the depths of the seas,
sources of rushing rivers: may all these
break into song as we sing to Father, Son
and Holy Spirit. May all the angels in
the heavens reply: Amen, Amen, Amen.
Power, praise, honour, eternal glory to
God, the only Giver of grace, Amen,
Amen, Amen.

Anonymous (3ʳᵈ–6ᵗʰ centuries)

PRAISE FOR SALVATION

Let us praise the Lord!

He will cause the bright dawn of salvation
    to rise on us
and to shine from heaven on all those who
    live in the dark shadow of death,
to guide our steps in the path of peace.

FROM THE PRAYER OF ZECHARIAH, THE FATHER OF
JOHN THE BAPTIST. LUKE 1:68, 78–79

MARY'S SONG OF PRAISE

My heart praises the Lord;
my soul is glad because of God my
 Saviour,
for he has remembered me, his lowly
 servant!
From now on all people will call me happy,
because of the great things the Mighty
 God has done for me.
His name is holy.

PART OF MARY'S SONG OF PRAISE, LUKE 1:46–49

YOU ARE MY GOD

You are holy, Lord, the only God,
  and your deeds are wonderful.
You are strong.
  You are great.
  You are the Most High,
  You are almighty.
  You, holy Father, are
  King of heaven and earth.
You are Three and One,
  Lord God, all good.
  You are Good, all Good, supreme Good,
  Lord God, living and true.
You are love,
  You are wisdom.
  You are humility,
  You are endurance.
  You are rest,
  You are peace.
  You are joy and gladness.
  You are justice and moderation.
  You are all our riches,
  And you suffice for us.

You are beauty.
   You are gentleness.
You are our protector,
   You are our guardian and defender.
   You are courage.
   You are our haven and our hope.
You are our faith,
   Our great consolation.
   You are our eternal life,
   Great and wonderful Lord,
   God almighty,
   Merciful Saviour.

St Francis of Assisi (1181–1226)

GLORY TO GOD

Our Lord and God! You are worthy to
   receive glory, honour and power.
For you created all things,
and by your will they were given existence
   and life.

Revelation 4:11

GREAT IS THE ONE

White are the wavetops,
White is the snow:
Great is the One
Who made all things below.

Green are the grasslands,
Green is the tree:
Great is the One
Who has made you and me.

Blue are the cornflowers,
Blue is the sky:
Great is the One
Who made all things on high.

Gold is the harvest,
Gold is the sun:
God is our Maker –
Great is the One.

A LIFE OF PRAISE

Holy is the Lord my God
and holy are his ways
and holy is the life that I will lead
to give him praise.

WITH ALL MY STRENGTH

I praise the Lord with all my soul,
my strength, my heart, my mind:
he blesses me with love and grace
and is for ever kind.

Based on Psalm 103:1–4

THE GOD OF ALL

Our God is the God of all,
The God of heaven and earth,
Of the sea and the rivers;
The God of the sun and of the moon and of all
the stars;
The God of the lofty mountains and of the
lowly valleys.
He has His dwelling around heaven and earth
and sea, and all that in them is.

St Patrick (389–461)

Forgiven and Forgiving

MAKING AMENDS

Making amends
is an uphill road
and stony is the way.
At the top of the hill
you will find the gate
to a bright new shining day.

CONFESSION

I told God everything:
I told God about all the wrong things
   I had done.
I gave up trying to pretend.
I gave up trying to hide.
I knew that the only thing to do was
   to confess.

And God forgave me.

BASED ON PSALM 32:5

TIIE JESUS PRAYER

God, have mercy on me, a sinner!

FROM LUKE 18:13

TAKE MY WRONGDOING

Take my wrongdoing
and throw it away,
down in the deep of the sea;
welcome me into your kingdom of love
for all of eternity.

BASED ON MICAH 7:18–20

SET ME FREE

Dear God,
The lies I told have grown like brambles,
and now I am trapped in a tangle of
thorns.

Dear God, I don't know what to do; I just
want to be free again to tell the truth.

A NEW BEGINNING

From the mud
a pure white flower

From the storm
a clear blue sky

As we pardon
one another

God forgives us
from on high.

SOPHIE PIPER

PRAYER FOR KINDNESS

Dear God,
In my heart I believe I have done no
wrong, yet I know that someone feels that
I have wronged them.

Help me to be both brave and kind
towards them, even though they are being
angry and spiteful.

Help me to rebuild respect and friendship
between us.

A REASON TO FORGIVE

"If you forgive others the wrongs they have done to you," said Jesus, "your Father in heaven will also forgive you."

But it would be foolish to lavish forgiveness on others if one were perfect.

If.

LEARNING TO FORGIVE

Maybe I will learn to forgive.

Given time.

Given space.

Given the example of those more generous in spirit.

PRAYER FOR COURAGE

Dear God,
Give us the courage to overcome anger
with love.

FORGIVING THOSE OF ILL WILL

O Lord, remember not only the men and
women of good will, but also those of ill will.
But do not remember all the suffering they
have inflicted on us; remember the fruits we
have borne, thanks to this suffering – our
comradeship, our loyalty, our courage, our
generosity, the greatness of heart which has
grown out of all this, and when they come to
judgment let all the fruits which we have borne
be their forgiveness.

PRAYER WRITTEN BY AN UNKNOWN PRISONER IN
RAVENSBRUCK CONCENTRATION CAMP AND LEFT BY THE
BODY OF A DEAD CHILD

ALWAYS FORGIVING

Seven
times seven
I freely forgive
and seven
times seventy more.
Lord, give me the grace
to forgive
and forgive,
again
and again
I implore.

Thanksgiving

FOR GOD'S LOVE AND CARE

Thank you, dear God, for all the good things with which you have blessed us.

Thank you for your love in good times; thank you for your unfailing love in difficult times.

Thank you for your promise to be with us always.

Amen.

FOR ALL I AM

Thank you, God,
that I can walk and run on the earth.
Thank you, God,
that I can dive and swim in the water.
Thank you, God,
that I can leap and fall through the air.
Thank you, God,
that I can do everything under the sun.

THE LORD IS GOOD TO ME

The Lord is good to me,
And so I thank the Lord
For giving me the things I need,
The sun, the rain, the appleseed.
The Lord is good to me.

ATTRIBUTED TO JOHN CHAPMAN,
AMERICAN PIONEER AND PLANTER OF ORCHARDS
(1774–1845)

FOR MY FAMILY

I give thanks for the people
who are my home:
we share a place to shelter;
we share our food;
we share our times of work
and play and rest.

May we provide one another
with love, encouragement,
respect, and wisdom:
through laughter and celebration,
through tears and troubled times.

May we be to one another
roof and walls,
floor and hearth,
windows and doors.

FOR MY HOME

Thank you, dear God, for the little place
that is my home – more special to me than
all the stars in the universe.

THE CORNERS OF THIS HOUSE

God bless the corners of this house,
And be the lintel blest,
And bless the hearth and bless the board,
And bless each place of rest,
And bless each door that opens wide
To stranger as to kin,
And bless each crystal window pane
That lets the starlight in,
And bless the rooftree overhead
And every sturdy wall.
The peace of man, the peace of God,
The peace of love on all.

IRISH BLESSING

FOR THOSE WHO HELP US

O God,
We give thanks for the goodhearted
people who love us and do good to us and
who show their mercy and kindness by
providing us with food and drink, house
and shelter when we are in trouble or in
need.

FROM A 1739 PRAYER BOOK

FOR THOSE WHO WORK

For all those who work
to make things that work
I give thanks, Lord, every day;
to those who are working
to keep those things working,
give patience and wisdom, I pray.

FOR THOSE I TAKE FOR GRANTED

O God,
Make me more mindful of all those who
support my life and my wellbeing.

Help me to notice the daily acts of kindness
done by friends and strangers alike.

Help me to remember the hours of work
that people do so that I can enjoy food,
water, heat, and light whenever I need it.

Help me to remember those who keep on
working when I can take my leisure.

And when I am asleep, O God, bless and
strengthen those who keep on working.

TABLE GRACES

Let us take a moment
To thank God for our food,
For friends around the table
And everything that's good.

Morning is here,
The board is spread,
Thanks be to God,
Who gives us bread.

ANONYMOUS

The bread is warm and fresh,
The water cool and clear.
Lord of all life, be with us,
Lord of all life, be near.

AFRICAN GRACE

We give thanks for our hunger,
We give thanks for our food,
We give thanks for enough of each
To do our bodies good.

Some hae meat, and canna eat,
And some wad eat that want it;
But we hae meat, and we can eat,
And sae the Lord be thankit.

THE SELKIRK GRACE, ROBERT BURNS (1759–96)

ALL KINDS OF THINGS

Dear God,
Thank you for things I have in abundance,
to enjoy with frivolity.

Thank you for the things of which I have
    enough,
to enjoy thoughtfully.

Thank you that there are things I lack
that keep me trusting in your many
    blessings.

SOPHIE PIPER

EVERYDAY BLESSINGS

Everyday blessings
include
but are not limited to
sunrise
birdsong
silence
chatter
weeds in flower
doing good for free
a word of praise
daring
surviving
food
the homeward road
an old chair
twilight
stars.

THE BICYCLE

I give thanks, O God, for the bicycle.

I thank you for the ingenuity of those who
invented it and the cleverness of those who
help keep mine in good repair.

I thank you for the places it has taken me
and the friends who have pedalled
alongside me.

I thank you for all the good things it has
brought me:
freedom,
fitness,
speed,
balance,
humility.

I thank you for my bicycle:
companion on life's ups and downs.

UNLIKELY BLESSINGS

I give thanks for unlikely blessings:

when possessions disappoint and break,
I see more clearly what is truly valuable;

when people disdain and exclude me,
I see more clearly how to be a good friend;

when time is lost in delays and
   complications,
I see more clearly the beauty I was rushing
   past;

when darkness gathers around me,
I see, though dimly, the safe path you lay
   before me.

GREAT THANKS

O God,
who made all,
great thanks:
especially for water
that slips into my cup
from crystal stream
and silver pool –
unhoarded treasure
giving life.

NOW AND EVERMORE

For blessings here
and those in store
we give thanks now
and evermore.

Wonders of Creation

WHY ARE WE HERE?

Here on the ancient rock of earth
I sit and watch the sky;
I feel the breeze that moves the trees
While stately clouds float by.
I wonder why our planet home
Spins round and round the sun
And what will last for ever
When earth's days all are done.

THE GLORY OF CREATION

O God, we thank you for this earth, our
home; for the wide sky and the blessed
sun, for the salt sea and the running water,
for the everlasting hills and the never-
resting winds, for trees and the common
grass underfoot.

We thank you for our senses by which
we hear the songs of birds, and see the
splendour of the summer fields, and taste
of the autumn fruits, and rejoice in the feel
of the snow, and smell the breath of the
spring.

Grant us a heart wide open to all this
beauty; and save our souls from being so
blind that we pass unseeing when even the
common thornbush is aflame with your
glory, O God our creator, who lives and
reigns for ever and ever.

WALTER RAUSCHENBUSCH (1861–1918)

AN ISLAND RETREAT

Delightful I think it to be
in the bosom of an isle
on the crest of a rock,
that I may see often
the calm of the sea.

That I may see its heavy waves
over the glittering ocean
as they chant a melody to their Father
on their eternal course.

That I may bless the Lord
who has power over all,
heaven with its crystal orders of angels,
earth, ebb, flood-tide.

St Columba at Iona

SOME GREAT GOODNESS

At end of night, the sky is dark.
Up from nowhere flies a spark
of burning gold. It starts a blaze
among the far horizon's haze;
a fire of red and amber bright
that sets each charcoal cloud alight
and turns the purple and the grey
into the pink and blue of day.
Then rises up the golden O
that shines from heaven to earth below
with power and warmth and light and love
from some great Goodness far above.

MARK ROBINSON

THIS SIMPLY LOVELY DAY

This simply lovely day –
·   I want to share it.
There is no beauty with which
   to compare it.
Each green, each blue,
   each changing hue –
I hardly understand
   how heav'n can spare it.

DIVERSE MAJESTY

I think of the diverse majesty
of all of the creatures on earth –
some with the power to terrify
and others that only bring mirth.
I think of their shapes and their colours,
their secret and curious ways,
and my heart seems to long for a language
to sing their Great Maker's praise.

BRIGHT AND BEAUTIFUL

All things bright and beautiful,
All creatures great and small,
All things wise and wonderful,
The Lord God made them all.

Mrs C. F. Alexander (1818–95)

FOR WILD THINGS

Thank you, dear God, for the wild birds
and their wild and noisy cry;

for the wild hills and the wild woods
where the wild wind whistles by;

for the wild weeds with their wild seeds
that wind all the earth around;

for the wonder of all of this wildness
where order and beauty are found.

A WOODLAND CATHEDRAL

The woods are God's own cathedral
with pillars that reach to the sky
and a faraway ceiling of fluttering leaves
where songbirds and angels fly.

WOODLAND PRAYERS

God has written the name of every tree
in the pattern of the bark.

Every tree writes its prayer to God
in the pattern of leaves against the sky.

GOD MADE US ALL

He prayeth best, who loveth best
All things both great and small;
For the dear God who loveth us,
He made and loveth all.

S. T. COLERIDGE (1772–1834)

LITTLE CREATURES

The little bugs that scurry,
The little beasts that creep
Among the grasses and the weeds
And where the leaves are deep:
All of them were made by God
As part of God's design.
Remember that the world is theirs,
Not only yours and mine.

THE CREATOR'S LOVE AND CARE

Who would make a tiny flower
so beautiful? It lasts an hour!
Then bloom then quickly fades away
before the setting of the day.

Who would make a tiny leaf
so intricate? Its life is brief:
a season in the summer sun
before its fluttering life is done.

The One who made both great and small,
who loves and cares for one and all
on land and water, sky and sea:
the One who loves and cares for me.

DOMESTIC ANIMALS

We give thanks for domestic animals.
Those creatures who can trust us enough
to come close. Those creatures who can
trust us enough to be true to themselves.

They approach us from the wild. They
approach us from the inner world. They
bring beauty and joy, comfort and peace.

For this miracle and for the lesson of this
miracle, we give thanks.

Amen.

MICHAEL LEUNIG

FOR MY CAT

The basket where my cat slept
is empty, and the house is mournful
in its quiet stillness.
Dear God, thank you for my dear pet,
who brought me comfort
in moments of loneliness
and warmth on chilly winter days.

VICTORIA TEBBS

A PRAYER FOR LITTLE TINY THINGS

A prayer for little tiny things
whose little life has flown:
may they be safe in God's great love –
they are God's very own.

SEASONS

Winter is the time forlorn
with golden leaf and silver thorn

Spring gives life and joy again
with golden sun and silver rain

Summer is the time of glee
with golden sand and silver sea

Autumn days are on the ebb
with golden fruit and silver web.

Give thanks for the living earth
More than gold or silver worth.

SPRINGTIME PRAISES

Bless the Lord of heaven above,
sing to God with thanks and love.

Praise him for the joyful spring,
bringing life to everything.

Praise him for the blossom trees,
birds and butterflies and bees.

Praise him for the cloud and rain,
and for sunshine once again.

Bless the Lord of heaven above,
sing to God with thanks and love.

SOPHIE PIPER

A SUMMER PRAYER

Let me drift like a seagull
up in the summer sky
feeling the air grow gold and warm
as the sun rises high.

Let me drift like a seagull
out on the sea so wide
feeling the ocean rise and fall
as the moon pulls the tide.

Let me drift through summer
down by the ocean shore
marvelling in God's creation
now and for evermore.

PIED BEAUTY

Glory be to God for dappled things –
For skies of couple-colour as a brinded cow;
For rose-moles all in stipple upon trout that
   swim;
Fresh-firecoal chestnut-falls; finches' wings;
Landscape plotted and pieced – fold, fallow,
   and plough;
And all trades, their gear and tackle and trim.

All things counter, original, spare, strange;
Whatever is fickle, freckled (who knows how?)
With swift, slow; sweet, sour; adazzle, dim;
He fathers-forth whose beauty is past change:
   Praise him.

GERARD MANLEY HOPKINS (1844–89)

WHEN WINTER COMES

Now the wind is coming,
Now the wind is strong,
Now the winter freezes
And the darkness will be long.
Now we see the starlight
In the midnight sky,
We know God is with us
And the angels are close by.

GOD OF THE YEARS

Thank you, God,
for the unchanging patterns
of the seasons:
the frosts of winter
melting into moist spring,
the rain-soaked buds
unfolding into bright summer,
the flowers fading and falling
in the autumn mist
leaving the year cold and bare,
lit by a pale sun
and the golden promise
of your unfailing love.

TEACH US TO RESPECT THE WORLD

We think the earth is ours.

We dig it, drill it, plough it, mine it, pave it, bomb it.

Then, from within the heart of things, the earth erupts, it shakes, it quakes, it burns, it floods.

May we learn to respect the earth, for it is shaped by forces greater than our own, and we should live in awe of them.

RESTORE THE PATTERNS

O God,
You set the patterns of the world –
summer and winter,
seedtime and harvest –
so that all living things may flourish.

But we have been greedy
for warmth in wintertime
cool air in summertime
harvest crops at seedtime
spring flowers as the year grows old.

Teach us to live peaceably with the world.
Let the patterns be restored
and bless us.

SOPHIE PIPER

SAVE THE WILD

God of the mountain,
God of the plain:
may the wild creatures
run freely again.

God of the forest,
God of the glade:
shelter the creatures in leafy green shade.

God of the harvest,
God of the seed:
may the world's creatures
have all that they need.

A GLIMPSE OF THE STARS

We give thanks for streetlamps that shine on our
    path,
but oh! for a glimpse of the stars
that wheel their way through the heavens above
with Jupiter, Venus and Mars.

We give thanks for pavements without ruts or
    holes,
but oh! for the smell of the earth,
the feel of tussocks and tree-roots and mud,
the planet that gave us our birth.

THE MAKER'S TUNE

Let us learn how the rivers dance:

let us watch how they trickle and surge,
how they fall and curl,
how they swirl and eddy.

Let us see how they dance according to
the rules God gave them; how they are
more obedient to their Maker than any of
humankind.

Let us learn from the rivers how to dance
to the Maker's tune.

KEEP ME A PLACE IN THIS OLD LAND

Save me a clean stream, flowing
to unpolluted seas;

lend me the bare earth, growing
untamed flowers and trees.

May I share safe skies
when I wake, every day,

with birds and butterflies?
Grant me a space where I can play

with water, rocks, trees, and sand;
lend me forests, rivers, hills, and sea.

Keep me a place in this old land,
somewhere to grow, somewhere to be.

JANE WHITTLE

EARTH MADE WHOLE

I cultivate my garden
and as carefully tend my soul
to fit myself for heaven
and to leave the earth made whole.

For a Better World

CALM, COURAGE, CHEERFULNESS

In the face of evil and wrongdoing
I will surely not be happy,
Nor will I let myself grow too sad.
Instead, I will choose to stand up for what
   is right
And I will face the future
With calm and courage and cheerfulness.

WE ARE ALL RELATED

Grandfather, Great Spirit:
All over the world the faces of living things
 are alike.
You have fashioned them with tenderness
 from the clay.
Look upon your children, that they may
 face the winds
and walk the good road to the day of quiet.
Grandfather, Great Spirit:
Fill us with the light of your wisdom.
Give us the strength to understand and the
 eyes to see.
Teach us to walk the soft earth as relatives
 to all that live.

SIOUX PRAYER

WE SHARE THE EARTH

We share the earth
we share the sky
we share the shining sea
with those we trust
with those we fear:
we are God's family.

POINTS OF VIEW

May we learn to appreciate different points
of view:

to know that the view from the hill is
   different from the view in the valley;
the view to the east is different from the
   view to the west;
the view in the morning is different from
   the view in the evening;
the view of a parent is different from the
   view of a child;
the view of a friend is different from the
   view of a stranger;
the view of humankind is different from
   the view of God.

May we all learn to see what is good, what
is true, what is worthwhile.

OUR FELLOW HUMAN BEINGS

O God,
We are all strangers in this world
and we are all travelling to your country.

So may we not treat anyone as a foreigner
   or an outsider,
but simply as a fellow human being
made in your image.

TOLERANCE

O God, help us not to despise or oppose
what we do not understand.

WILLIAM PENN (1644–1718)

FOR MINORITIES

Dear God,
We pray for minorities: for the little groups
of people whose needs are overlooked;
the people whose voices are not heard;
the people who do not have much power.

Help us to find ways to help them in our
community. Help us to find ways to make
the government notice them. Help us to
work for justice in our own country.

THE BLESSING OF OLD AND NEW

Thank you, dear God,
for the blessing of things that stay the
    same:
for people we have known for ever
and the familiar paths where we walk.

Thank you, dear God,
for the blessing of things that change:
for newcomers with their new customs,
new ways of doing things, new paths to
    discover.

Thank you, dear God,
for the blessing of the old and the blessing
    of the new.

THE MAN ON THE PAVEMENT

The man on the pavement was shivering,
  Lord,
the man, he was shivering with cold;
the frost in the air made his hair look grey,
his eyes were sunken and old.

I didn't know what I should do, dear Lord,
and still don't know what I can give
to help that man get up and walk away
to where he can laugh and live.

STOPPING TO HELP

Dear God,
When I see someone in trouble,
may I know when to stop and help
and when to hurry to fetch help;
but may I never pass by,
pretending I did not see.

PRAYERS BASED ON JESUS' PARABLE OF THE
GOOD SAMARITAN, LUKE 10:25–37

A CITY PILGRIM

I am a city pilgrim:
with God I walk the street,
looking for the face of Christ
in everyone I meet.

WAITING FOR GOD'S JUSTICE

O God,
How long must I call for help before you listen?
How can you let this wrongdoing go on…
all the fighting and the quarrelling?
Wicked people are getting the better of good
people; it is not right, it is not fair!

I will wait quietly for God to bring justice.
Even in the middle of disaster I will be joyful,
because God is my saviour.

BASED ON THE BOOK OF HABAKKUK

FOR THOSE CONDEMNED AS WICKED

We pray for the people who are condemned as
wicked: those who are responsible for wars and
massacres and terrorism.

We pray that people of good faith will find a
way to stop them.

We also pray that you and we will treat them
with justice and mercy.

FOR THE CASUALTIES OF WAR

Dear God,
We pray for the casualties of war:

for the young and the old,
for the parents and the children;

for the birds and the animals,
for the fields and the flowers;

for the earth and the water,
for the sea and the sky.

We pray for their healing.

SETTLE THE QUARRELS

O God,
Settle the quarrels among the nations.

May they hammer their swords into ploughs
and their spears into pruning knives…

Where the tanks now roll, let there be tractors;
where the landmines explode, let the fields grow
 crops.

Let there be a harvest of fruit and grain
and peace that all the world can share.

BASED ON MICAH 4:3–5

THE OLIVE TREE

The olive tree I thought was dead
has opened new green leaves instead
and where the landmines tore the earth
now poppies dance with joy and mirth.

The doves build nests, they coo and sigh
beside the field where corn grows high
and grapes hang heavy on the vine,
and those who fought share bread and
    wine.

THE GOOD SHEPHERD

This is what God says:

"I myself will look for my people and take care of them in the same way as shepherds take care of their sheep.

"I will bring them back from all the places where they were scattered on that dark, disastrous day.

"I will lead them to the mountains and the streams of their own land, so they may make their home amid the green pastures.

"I shall be their God, their Good Shepherd; they will be my people, my flock."

FROM EZEKIEL 34

114

FOR REFUGEES

Lord, watch over refugees,
their tired feet aching.
Help them bear their heavy loads,
their backs breaking.
May they find a place of rest,
no fears awake them.
May you always be their guide,
never forsake them.

SEND HEALING RAIN

There's trouble in the fields, Lord,
The crops are parched and dry.
We water them with tears, Lord,
So help us, hear our cry.

There's trouble in our hearts, Lord,
The world is full of pain.
Set us to work for healing,
Send blessings down like rain.

BLESS THOSE WHO WORK THE FIELDS

Lord, help those who plant and sow,
weed and water, rake and hoe,
toiling in the summer heat
for the food they need to eat.

Bless the work of their tired hands:
turn their dry and dusty lands
to a garden, green and gold,
as their harvest crops unfold.

MAKING FRIENDS

We
not me.

Share
not tear.

Mend
not end

and so
befriend.

GATHER US AS ONE

O God,
Gather together as one
those who believe in peace.
Gather together as one
those who believe in justice.
Gather together as one
those who believe in love.

PRAYER FOR CHANGE

May the world turn round about,
may all things turn to right;
may the sunset thank the dawn,
the noontime bless the night;

May the rivers thank the rain,
the stormclouds bless the sea;
may the good soil thank the leaves,
the sunshine bless the tree;

May the rich thank those in need,
the children bless the old;
may the strong thank those who fail,
the timid bless the bold;

May the angels sing on earth,
may heaven hear our prayer;
may forgiveness, joy and peace
and love fill everywhere.

GOD'S ENDURING LOVE

Dear God,
When everything is going wrong I
sometimes wonder why you let bad things
happen.

But then you open my eyes to the majesty
of your world, and I know once more that
your are far greater than I can imagine,
and I believe once more that your love and
goodness will not be overcome.

BASED ON THE BOOK OF JOB

Following the Way

THE PRAYER JESUS TAUGHT

Our Father in heaven,
hallowed be your name,
your kingdom come,
your will be done,
on earth as in heaven.
Give us today our daily bread.
Forgive us our sins
as we forgive those who sin against us.
Lead us not into temptation
but deliver us from evil.

For the kingdom, the power,
and the glory are yours
now and for ever.
Amen.

THE BEATITUDES

Blessed are the poor in spirit, for theirs is the kingdom of heaven.

Blessed are those who mourn, for they will be comforted.

Blessed are the meek, for they will inherit the earth.

Blessed are those who hunger and thirst for righteousness, for they will be filled.

Blessed are the merciful, for they will receive mercy.

Blessed are the pure in heart, for they will see God.

Blessed are the peacemakers, for they will be called children of God.

Blessed are those who are persecuted for righteousness' sake, for theirs is the kingdom of heaven.

FROM MATTHEW 5:3–10

THE WAY OF THE LORD

Lord, make us to walk in your way:
"Where there is love and wisdom, there is
neither fear nor ignorance;
where there is patience and humility,
there is neither anger nor annoyance;
where there is poverty and joy, there is neither
greed nor avarice;
where there is peace and contemplation,
there is neither care nor restlessness;
where there is the fear of God to guard the
dwelling, there no enemy can enter;
where there is mercy and prudence, there is
neither excess nor harshness";
this we know through your Son, Jesus Christ
our Lord.

SAINT FRANCIS OF ASSISI (1181–1226)

OPEN MY EYES

Open my eyes
so I can see
the ways I could
more useful be.

Give me the strength
and heart and mind
to do the things
that are good and kind.

IN GOD'S PRESENCE

Who may come into God's presence?

The person who obeys God in everything,
who always speaks the truth,
who keeps every promise,
who cannot be lured into doing wrong.

Such a person will be safe all through life.

FROM PSALM 15

KEEPING THE COMMANDMENTS

O Lord,
I have heard your laws.

May I worship you.

May I worship you alone.

May all I say and do show respect for your
holy name.

May I honour the weekly day of rest.

May I show respect for my parents.

May I reject violence so that I never take
a life.

May I learn to be loyal in friendship and
so learn to be faithful in marriage.

May I not steal what belongs to others.

May I not tell lies to destroy another person's reputation.

May I not be envious of what others have, but may I learn to be content with the good things you give me.

BASED ON THE TEN COMMANDMENTS, EXODUS 20

A SAFE PATHWAY

God makes me strong
and keeps my pathway safe;
he makes me sure-footed as a deer
on the perilous mountainside.

From Psalm 18

DO NOT FOLLOW THE WICKED

Do not follow the advice of the wicked,
but obey every word of God.

For the wicked are nothing more than
wisps of straw in the autumn gale; but the
righteous are like trees that grow by the
lifegiving river, bearing leaves and fruit in
their season.

From Psalm 1

TEACH ME

Teach me, O God,
to do what is just,
to show constant love
and to live in fellowship with you.

BASED ON MICAH 6:8

THE NARROW PATH

I will choose the narrow path,
I will walk the straight,
Through the wide and winding world
Up to heaven's gate.

I AM A PILGRIM

I am a pilgrim on a journey
to the place where God is found;
every step along that journey
is upon God's holy ground.

CHRIST BE WITH ME

Christ be with me
Christ within me
Christ behind me
Christ before me
Christ beside me
Christ to win me
Christ to comfort and restore me
Christ beneath me
Christ above me
Christ in quiet and
Christ in danger
Christ in hearts of all that love me
Christ in mouth of friend and stranger.

St Patrick (389–461)

AN ANGEL TO GUIDE ME

May angels guide me through this day;
the paths unknown, but blessed the way.

SOPHIE PIPER

AN ANGEL TO WATCH ME

I will live this day thoughtfully so that, if
my guardian angel were to give an account
of it, I would not be ashamed.

FROM THE RESOLUTIONS OF ST CONRAD OF
PARZHAM (1818–94)

COMMITTED TO GOODNESS

May I be no one's enemy, and may I be the friend of that which lasts for ever.

May I never quarrel with those nearest: and if I do, may I be quick to restore the friendship.

May I love only what is good: always seek it and work to achieve it.

May I wish for everyone to find happiness and not envy anyone their good fortune.

May I never gloat when someone who has wronged me suffers ill fortune.

When I have done or said something wrong, may I not wait to be told off, but instead be angry with myself until I have put things right.

May I win no victory that harms either me or those who compete against me.

May I help those who have quarrelled to be friends with each other again.

May I, as far as I can, give practical help to my friends and anyone who is in need.

May I never fail a friend who is in danger.

When I visit those who are grieving, may I find the right words to help heal their pain.

May I respect myself.

May I always control my emotions.

May I train myself to be gentle and not allow myself to become angry.

May I never whisper about wicked people and the things they have done, but rather seek to spend my time with good people and to follow their good example.

EUSEBIUS (3ʳᵈ CENTURY, ADAPTED)

AN INSTRUMENT OF YOUR PEACE

Lord, make me an instrument of your
  peace.
Where there is hatred, let me sow love,
Where there is injury, pardon,
Where there is doubt, faith,
Where there is despair, hope,
Where there is darkness, light,
Where there is sadness, joy.

O divine Master, grant that I may not so
much seek to be consoled as to console,
not so much to be understood as to
understand, not so much to be loved as to
love; for it is in giving that we receive, it is
in pardoning that we are pardoned, it is in
dying that we awake to eternal life.

A PRAYER ASSOCIATED WITH ST FRANCIS OF ASSISI
(1181–1226)

FAITH, HOPE, LOVE

Help me, Lord, to show your love.

Help me to be patient and kind, not jealous or conceited or proud. May I never be ill-mannered, selfish or irritable; may I be quick to forgive and forget.

May I not gloat over wrongdoing, but rather be glad about things that are good and true.

May I never give up loving; may my faith and hope and patience never come to an end.

BASED ON 1 CORINTHIANS 13:4–7

ALL MY DEEDS

May all my deeds
be wheat
not weeds.

SOPHIE PIPER

THE BEST THINGS

May I do the best things
in the worst times
and hope them
in the most calamitous.

INSPIRED BY A CHURCH INSCRIPTION IN PRAISE
OF SIR ROBERT SHIRLEY IN STAUNTON HAROLD
CHURCH, LEICESTERSHIRE

DOING GOOD JOYFULLY

I am resolved this day to be
a friend of love and liberty
in service and humility
with joy and great hilarity.

DOING GOOD IN SMALL THINGS

We can do no great things,
Only small things with great love.

BLESSED TERESA OF CALCUTTA (1910–97)

DOING GOD'S WILL

Teach us, Lord,
to serve you as you deserve,
to give and not to count the cost,
to fight and not to heed the wounds,
to toil and not to seek for rest,
to labour and not to ask for any reward
save that of knowing that we do your will.

St Ignatius Loyola (1491–1556)

DAY BY DAY

Day by day,
dear Lord, of thee
three things I pray:
to see thee more clearly,
love thee more dearly,
follow thee more nearly,
day by day.

RICHARD, BISHOP OF CHICHESTER (1197–1253)

THE HILL OF THE TWO WINDS

I walk the hill of the two winds:
from the south comes gentleness and
warmth;
from the north, bitterness and cold.

May I keep south wind at my back, urging
me to my rightful destination;

may the north wind in my face not destroy
my resolve.

May I walk the hill of the two winds
to my journey's end.

GIVE ME STRENGTH AND WISDOM

O Great Spirit, whose voice I hear in the wind,
Whose breath gives life to all the world:
Hear me. I need your strength and wisdom.
Let me walk in beauty.
Open my eyes to see the wonders of the earth
  and the heavens.
Make my hands respect the things you have
  made,
and my ears sharp to hear your voice.
Keep my thoughts centred on what is good and
  lovely.
Give me the strength to help others with
  gladness and humility.
Make me always ready to come to you
with clean hands and straight eyes.

A PRAYER FROM THE NAVAJO TRADITION

GOD WILL TAKE CARE OF ME

God feeds the birds that sing from the
   treetops;
God feeds the birds that wade by the sea;
God feeds the birds that dart through the
   meadows;
So will God take care of me?

God clothes the flowers that bloom on the
   hillside;
God clothes the blossom that hangs from
   the tree;
As God cares so much for the birds and
   the flowers
I know God will take care of me.

A PRAYER BASED ON JESUS' SERMON ON THE
MOUNT, MATTHEW 6

TRUE RICHES

Grant me riches
here on earth –
things that are
of priceless worth:

The shining sun
the silver sea
the diamond rain
the emerald tree.

For better far
than any gold
these treasure are
that none can hold.

LIVE WITH LESS

Learn to lend the things you own,
Learn to live with less,
Learn to look to a further shore
And God your life will bless.

SPIRIT OF GOD

Spirit of God
put love in my life.

Spirit of God
put joy in my life.

Spirit of God
put peace in my life.

Spirit of God
make me patient.

Spirit of God
make me kind.

Spirit of God
make me good.

Spirit of God
give me faithfulness.

Spirit of God
give me humility.

Spirit of God
give me self-control.

FROM GALATIANS 5:22–23

GROWING IN GODLINESS

To faith, let me add goodness;
to goodness, let me add knowledge;
to knowledge, let me add self-control;
to self-control, let me add endurance;
to endurance, let me add godliness;
to godliness, let me add affection for my
  brothers and sisters;
to affection, let me add love.

FROM 2 PETER 1:5–7

When Trouble Comes

AS THE RAIN HIDES THE STARS

As the rain hides the stars,
as the autumn mist hides the hills,
as the clouds veil the blue of the sky,
so the dark happenings of my lot
hide the shining of your face from me.
Yet, if I may hold your hand in the darkness,
it is enough.
Since I know that,
though I may stumble in my going,
you do not fall.

GAELIC PRAYER
(TRANSLATED BY ALISTAIR MacLean)

ALL THINGS WORK TOGETHER

Dear God,
You can make all things work together for
the good.
Take this moment of failure and
disappointment
and make it part of my journey to wisdom
and happiness.

AT PEACE

Lord, I have given up my pride
  and turned away from my arrogance.
I am not concerned with great matters
  or with subjects too difficult for me.
Instead, I am content and at peace.
As a child lies quietly in its mother's arms,
  so my heart is quiet within me.

PSALM 131:1–2

IN OUR TROUBLES

Thank you, God, that you help us in our
troubles, so that we can help others who
have all kinds of troubles.

FROM 2 CORINTHIANS 1:4

I WILL TRUST GOD ALWAYS

My Lord God, I have no idea where I am going. I do not see the road ahead of me. I cannot know for certain where it will end… Therefore I will trust you always though I may seem to be lost and in the shadow of death. I will not fear for you are ever with me, and you will never leave me to face my perils alone.

Anonymous

I WILL NOT WORRY

I will not worry,
dear God,
but I will ask you for the things I need
and give thanks.

Give me the peace that comes from knowing
that all my worries are safe with you.

FROM PHILIPPIANS 4:6–7

MY LIGHT AND MY SALVATION

The Lord is my light and my salvation;
I will fear no one.
The Lord protects me from all danger;
I will never be afraid.

PSALM 27:1

DO NOT ABANDON ME

My God, my God, why have you abandoned me?
I have cried desperately for help, but still it does
    not come.

It was you who brought me safely through birth,
    and when I was a baby, you kept me safe.
I have relied on you since the day I was born,
    and you have always been my God.
Do not stay away from me!
    Trouble is near, and there is no one to help.

O Lord, don't stay away from me!
    Come quickly to my rescue!

PSALM 22:1,9–11, 19

SHELTER AND STRENGTH

God is our shelter and strength,
  always ready to help in times of trouble.
So we will not be afraid, even if the earth
    is shaken
  and mountains fall into the ocean
    depths;
even if the seas roar and rage,
  and the hills are shaken by the violence.

PSALM 46:1–3

THE LORD IS MY SHEPHERD

The Lord is my shepherd;
   I have everything I need.
He lets me rest in fields of green grass
   and leads me to quiet pools of fresh
      water.
He gives me new strength.
He guides me in the right paths,
   as he has promised.
Even if I go through the deepest darkness,
   I will not be afraid, Lord,
     for you are with me.
Your shepherd's rod and staff protect me.

You prepare a banquet for me,
    where all my enemies can see me;
you welcome me as an honoured guest
    and fill my cup to the brim.
I know that your goodness and love will be
    with me all my life;
    and your house will be my home as long
        as I live.

PSALM 23

A DARK ROOM

My room is dark
in deepest night:
O fill my life
with heaven's light.

I am awake
to unknown fear:
O send the angels
very near.

Then let me
softly fall asleep
till sunbeams
through the window creep.

AWAKE IN THE NIGHT

Father God,
I am awake in the night,
and all alone,
like so many others.
Some are afraid: give them courage.
Some are worried: give them hope.
Some are sad: give them comfort.
Some are just tired: give them sleep.

HEALING SLEEP

Dear God, let me sleep the aching away.
Dear God, let me sleep the weakness away.
Dear God, let me sleep the tiredness away.
Dear God, let me sleep the long hours away.

SOUL BALM

Give us, O God, the needs the body feels,
Give us, God, the need-things of the soul;
Give us, O God, the balm which body
   heals,
Give us, God, the soul-balm which makes
   whole.

POEMS OF THE WESTERN HIGHLANDERS

WATCH OVER US

Keep watch, dear Lord, with those who work, or watch, or weep this night, and give your angels charge over those who sleep.

Tend the sick, Lord Christ; give rest to the weary, bless the dying, soothe the suffering, pity the afflicted, shield the joyous; and all for your love's sake.

ST AUGUSTINE (354 430)

WALKING WITH JESUS

Jesus, who walked to the cross,
be with us when we feel abandoned.

Jesus, who walked to the cross,
be with us when we face danger.

Jesus, who walked to the cross,
be with us when we are suffering.

When sorrow threatens to defeat us,
Jesus, who rose from the dead, be with us.

MAKE ALL THINGS NEW

O God,
Put an end to death.
Put an end to grief and crying and pain.
Make all things new.
Lead us to heaven.

FROM REVELATION 21

REMEMBERING

Every day
in silence we remember

those whom we loved
to whom we have said a last goodbye.

Every day
in silence we remember.

GIVE WINGS TO MY SOUL

Give wings to my soul,
O God,
that I may fly away from the icy wind,
that I may escape the winter's dark.

Guide me on paths invisible
to a new land
that will be my home.

MAKE FOR ME AN ARK

O God,
make for me an ark to float upon the water
and carry me through the swirling flood.

O God,
make for me a road through the wilderness
and lead me to a place of safety.

O God,
send me a light in the darkness
and bring me to the beginning of a new day.

WALK WITH ME

Walk with me in golden sun
Walk with me in rain
Walk with me in happiness
Walk with me in pain.

Walk with me at morning time
When the world is light
Walk with me when darkness comes
Watch me through the night.

AN END TO SORROW

Come, O Joy:
Let heaven break into my dark night of
sorrow like the early dawn of a summer
morning.

SHELTER ME

O God,
be to me
like the evergreen tree
and shelter me in your shade,
and bless me again
like the warm gentle rain
that gives life to all you have made.

BASED ON HOSEA 14:4–8

HOW CAN I KEEP FROM SINGING?

My life flows on in endless song;
Above earth's lamentation
I hear the sweet though far-off hymn
That hails a new creation:
Through all the tumult and the strife
I hear the music ringing;
It finds an echo in my soul –
How can I keep from singing?

What though my joys and comforts die?
The Lord my Saviour liveth;
What though the darkness gather round!
Songs in the night he giveth:
No storm can shake my inmost calm
While to that refuge clinging;
Since Christ is Lord of heaven and earth,
how can I keep from singing?

ROBERT LOWRY (1826–99)

JUST FOR TODAY

Lord, for tomorrow and its needs,
I do not pray;
But keep me, guide me, love me, Lord,
Just for today.

SISTER M XAVIER (1856–1917)

AMEN AND ALLELUIA

All shall be Amen and Alleluia.
We shall rest and we shall see.
We shall see and we shall know.
We shall know and we shall love.
We shall love and we shall praise.
Behold our end which is no end.

St Augustine (354–430)

Festivals of the
Christian Year

ALL AROUND THE YEAR

Harvest time is gold and red:
Thank you, God, for daily bread.
Christmas time is red and green:
Heaven now on earth is seen.
Easter time is green and white:
Bring us all to heaven's light.
Pentecost is white and gold:
God's own spirit makes us bold.

CELEBRATING THE BIRTH

We celebrate the birth of Jesus:
for God has come among us.

We celebrate the birth of Jesus:
for heaven has come to earth.

We celebrate the birth of Jesus:
and let love grow between us.

We celebrate the birth of Jesus:
and live as God's children on earth.

SOPHIE PIPER

LOVE FROM HEAVEN

Christmas is
about a birth:
a child from heaven
and peace on earth.

Christmas is
about a night
transformed by heaven's
shining light.

Christmas is
about God's love
that reaches down
from heaven above.

So we pray
this Christmas morn
that peace and love
and light will dawn.

CELEBRATING CHRISTMAS

God, our loving Father, help us remember the
birth of Jesus, that we may share in the song of
the angels, the gladness of the shepherds and
the wisdom of the wise men.

Close the door of hate and open the door of love
all over the world.

Deliver us from evil by the blessing which
Christ brings and teach us to be merry with
clean hearts.

May the Christmas morning make us happy
to be your children and the Christmas evening
bring us to our beds with grateful thoughts,
forgiving and forgiven, for Jesus' sake. Amen.

ROBERT LOUIS STEVENSON (1850–94)

CHRISTMAS BLESSINGS FOR ALL

Let us remember Mary this Christmas
And may God bless our mothers.

Let us remember Joseph this Christmas
And may God bless our fathers.

Let us remember Elizabeth and Zechariah and
  John this Christmas
And may God bless all our relatives.

Let us remember the shepherds this Christmas
And may God bless all those who will be
  working.

Let us remember the wise men this Christmas
And may God bless all those who will be
  travelling.

Let us remember Jesus this Christmas
And may God bless us all and make us his
  children.

PEACE ON EARTH

This Christmas the night sky will be all aflame
and shepherds will cower in fear
when they see the anti-aircraft fire
and know enemy planes are near.

The light and the fire will tell out the news
of ill will and war on earth
and bombs will rain down near the humble
  room
where a mother has just given birth.

And so, let us pray for a miracle
of one holy, silent night
and ask God to give us the wisdom we need
to help put the world to right.

CHRISTMAS GIFTS

Lord Jesus,
The wise men brought you gold:
Let us use our riches to do good.

The wise men brought you frankincense:
Let our prayers rise like smoke to heaven.

The wise men brought you myrrh:
Let us seek to comfort those who are sad
  and grieving.

Lord Jesus,
You have given use so many rich gifts:
Let us use them to do your work in this
  world.

HUNTING FOR CHRISTMAS

You can hunt for Christmas:
tempt it with food,
entice it with gifts,
set a snare of tinsel and ribbon;
but you cannot catch it
by such stratagems.
You must wait
in a circle of love
lit by starlight
for Christmas
to find you.

CHRISTMAS ALL YEAR LONG

Let there be little Christmasses
throughout the year,
when unexpected acts of kindness
bring heaven's light to earth.

GOOD FRIDAY

Blessed be the name of Jesus, who died to
   save us.
Blessed be Jesus, who had compassion on us.
Blessed be Jesus, who suffered loneliness,
   rejection and pain, for our sakes.
Blessed be Jesus, through whose cross I am
   forgiven.
Lord Jesus, deepen my understanding of
   your suffering and death.

WRITTEN BY YOUNG PEOPLE IN KENYA

SUFFERING AND HEALING

Lord Jesus, who died upon the cross:
You know this world's suffering,
You know this world's sorrowing,
You know this world's dying.

Lord Jesus, who rose again, in your name
I will work for this world's healing,
I will work for this world's rejoicing,
I will work for this world's living.

EASTER ANGELS

Come, Holy Angels,
into this dark night.
Roll away the stone of death.
Let the light of life
shine from heaven.

EASTER IS ABOUT...

Good Friday is about
burdens loaded on innocent shoulders
and nails hammered into innocent hands,
a spear piercing an innocent heart
and death enshrouding an innocent life.

Easter is about
unexpected and joyful reunions
and simple meals shared with friends,
old grievances forgiven and forgotten
and angels rolling wide the way to heaven.

REJOICE AT EASTER

The whole bright world rejoices now:
with laughing cheer! with boundless joy!
The birds do sing on every bough:
Alleluia!

Then shout beneath the racing skies:
with laughing cheer! with boundless joy!
To him who rose that we might rise:
Alleluia!

God, Father, Son and Holy Ghost:
with laughing cheer! with boundless joy!
Our God most high, our joy, our boast:
Alleluia!

EASTER CAROL (17TH CENTURY)

THE EASTER TREE

The tree of thorns
is dressed in white
for resurrection day;
and joy springs from
the underworld
now death is put away.

Lord, make my life
grow like a tree
from earth to heaven above,
and by your Spirit
bear the fruits
of peace and joy and love.

DOUBT AND FAITH

We celebrate Easter with the disciples who
  saw the risen Jesus,
and who knew that love was stronger than
  death.

We also remember Thomas, for whom
  Easter was a long time coming,
and all those who feel alone in their doubt
  and despair this Easter.

Risen Jesus, make yourself known to us all
  in due time
so we may know for sure the joy of heaven.

EASTER PRAISES

Spring has come with chrysoprase
and tourmaline and gold:
from the earth the daffodils
and primroses unfold.

Life has risen from the clay
and hope is on the wing;
so to the One who gives us life
my Easter praise I'll sing.

A PRAYER FOR ASCENSION DAY

Christ has no body now on earth but yours,
no hands but yours, no feet but yours…
Yours are the feet with which he is to go
   about doing good,
and yours are the hands with which he is to
   bless us now.

St Teresa of Avila (1515–82)

A PRAYER FOR PENTECOST

Let the Spirit come
like the winds that blow:
take away my doubts;
help my faith to grow.

Let the Spirit come
like a flame of gold:
warm my soul within;
make me strong and bold.

A HARVEST PSALM

We plough the land,
God sends the rain
to bring the harvest
once again;
and when the fields
of wheat turn gold,
then God's great goodness
must be told.

Based on Psalm 65

ABUNDANT HARVESTS

We harvest the fields,
we harvest the trees,
we harvest the gardens,
we harvest the seas.

We gather the blessings
that God freely gives
to you and to me
and to each one who lives.

FOR THE HARVEST OF THE WILD

Thank you for the orchard,
thank you for the field,
thank you for the garden
and the harvest yield.

Thank you for the wild wood
where nuts and berries fall
and for the wild harvest
for wild creatures all.

A PRAYER FOR ADVENT

The days are dark.
Dear God, give us your true light.

The days are dark.
Dear God, give us your true life.

The days are dark.
Dear God, give us your true love.

WAITING FOR CHRISTMAS

When I walk in darkness
let me see the Christmas star
may it shine upon my path
though the way be far.

Let me see that Christmas star
guiding through the night;
let me travel hopefully
to the dawning light.

At Close of Day

SAFE THIS NIGHT

Lord, keep us safe this night,
Secure from all our fears;
May angels guard us while we sleep,
Till morning light appears.

John Leland (1754–1841)

NOW I LAY ME DOWN TO SLEEP

Now I lay me down to sleep,
I pray thee, Lord, thy child to keep;
Thy love to guard me through the night
and wake me in the morning light.

Traditional

EVENING (IN WORDS OF ONE SYLLABLE)

The day is past, the sun is set,
  And the white stars are in the sky;
While the long grass with dew is wet,
  And through the air the bats now fly.

The lambs have now lain down to sleep,
  The birds have long since sought their
    nests;
The air is still; and dark, and deep
  On the hill side the old wood rests.

Yet of the dark I have no fear,
  But feel as safe as when 'tis light;
For I know God is with me there,
  And He will guard me through the
    night.

For God is by me when I pray,
  And when I close mine eyes in sleep,
I know that He will with me stay,
  And will all night watch by me keep.

For He who rules the stars and sea,
　Who makes the grass and trees to grow,
Will look on a poor child like me,
　When on my knees I to Him bow.

He holds all things in His right hand,
　The rich, the poor, the great, the small;
When we sleep, or sit, or stand,
　Is with us, for He loves us all.

Thomas Miller (1807–74)

DAY IS DONE

The day is done;
O God the Son,
Look down upon
Thy little one!

O Light of Light,
Keep me this night,
And shed round me
Thy presence bright.

I need not fear
If Thou are near;
Thou art my Saviour
Kind and dear.

AUTHOR UNKNOWN

TODAY, TONIGHT, AND FOR EVER

O God,
Be thou a bright flame before me,
Be thou a guiding star above me,
Be thou a smooth path below me,
And be a kindly shepherd behind me,
Today, tonight, and for ever.

FROM CARMINA GADELICA

SEND ME SLEEP

Lord, send me sleep that I may live;
The wrongs I've done this day forgive.
Bless every deed and thought and word
I've rightly done, or said, or heard.
Bless relatives and friends alway;
Teach all the world to watch and pray.
My thanks for all my blessings take
And hear my prayer for Jesus' sake.

AUTHOR UNKNOWN

ALL THOSE THAT I LOVE

God bless all those that I love;
God bless all those that love me;
God bless all those that love those that
   I love,
And all those that love those that love me.

FROM AN OLD SAMPLER

PRAISE IN THE NIGHT

I sing a song of praise to God
throughout the darkest night,
for guarding me, for guiding me
to know what's good and right.
No evil things will frighten me,
no shadows from the tomb,
for God is light and life and power
to scatter midnight's gloom.

BASED ON PSALM 16:7–11

KEEP US SAFE FROM HARM

Guard us through the night, dear God,
and keep us safe from harm;
from all our wild imaginings
and every false alarm.

GOOD LORD DELIVER US

From ghoulies and ghosties
Long-leggety beasties
And things that go bump in the night,
Good Lord deliver us.

TRADITIONAL CORNISH PRAYER

GRACE, LOVE, FAVOUR

May the grace of Christ our Saviour,
And the Father's boundless love,
With the Holy Spirit's favour,
Rest upon us from above.

JOHN NEWTON (1725–1807)

GLORY TO THEE, MY GOD

Glory to thee, my God, this night,
For all the blessings of the light;
Keep me, O keep me, King of kings,
Beneath thine everlasting wings.

Praise God from whom all blessings flow;
Praise him, all creatures here below;
Praise him above, ye heavenly host;
Praise Father, Son, and Holy Ghost.

BISHOP THOMAS KEN (1637 1711)

NOW THE DAY IS OVER

Now the day is over,
  Night is drawing nigh.
Shadows of the evening
  Steal across the sky.

Now the darkness gathers,
  Stars begin to peep,
Birds and beasts and flowers
  Soon will be asleep.

Jesu, give the weary
  Calm and sweet repose;
With thy tenderest blessing
  May our eyelids close.

Through the long night-watches
  May thine angels spread
Their white wings above me,
  Watching round my bed.

When the morning wakens,
  Then may I arise,
Pure, and fresh, and sinless
  In thy holy eyes.

Glory to the Father,
  Glory to the Son,
And to thee, blest Spirit
  Whilst all ages run.

SABINE BARING-GOULD (1834–1924)

DAY IS DONE

Day is done,
Gone the sun
From the lake,
From the hills,
From the sky.
Safely rest,
All is well!
God is nigh.

ANONYMOUS

IN PEACEFUL TRUST

Send your peace into my heart, O Lord,
that I may be contented with your mercies
   of this day
and confident of your protection for this
   night;
and having forgiven others,
even as you forgive me,
may I go to my rest in peaceful trust
through Jesus Christ, our Lord, Amen.

ST FRANCIS OF ASSISI (1181–1226)

GAELIC BLESSING

Deep peace of the running waves to you,
Deep peace of the flowing air to you,
Deep peace of the quiet earth to you,
Deep peace of the shining stars to you,
Deep peace of the shades of night to you,
Moon and stars always giving light to you,
Deep peace of Christ, the Son of Peace,
   to you.

TRADITIONAL GAELIC BLESSING

BIBLE BLESSING

May the Lord bless you,
may the Lord take care of you;
May the Lord be kind to you,
may the Lord be gracious to you;
May the Lord look on you with favour,
may the Lord give you peace.

From Numbers 6:24–26

INDEX OF FIRST LINES